The Ultimate Guide to Wrestling Nutrition: Maximize Your Potential

By

Joseph Correa

Certified Sports Nutritionist

COPYRIGHT

© 2014 Correa Media Group

All rights reserved

Reproduction or translation of any part of this work beyond that permitted by section 107

or 108 of the 1976 United States Copyright Act without the permission of the copyright owner is unlawful.

This publication is designed to provide accurate and authoritative information in regard to the subject matter covered. It is sold with the understanding that neither the author nor the publisher is engaged in rendering medical advice. If medical advice or assistance is needed, consult with a doctor. This book is considered a guide and should not be used in any way detrimental to your health. Consult with a physician before starting this nutritional plan to make sure it's right for you.

ACKNOWLEDGEMENTS

The realization and success of this book could not have been possible without the motivation and support of my family.

The Ultimate Guide to Wrestling Nutrition: Maximize Your Potential

By

Joseph Correa

Certified Sports Nutritionist

CONTENTS

Copyright

Acknowledgements

About The Author

WHY THIS NUTRITION GUIDE?

INTRODUCTION

Motivation by Necessity

CHAPTER 1: The Ultimate Guide to Wrestling Nutrition: Maximize your potential

CHAPTER 2: Eat, Sleep, Breathe Your Way to a Leaner Body

Your secret weapon RMR

CHAPTER 3: How to Get in Shape 24 Hours a Day

Accelerating your metabolism to enhance performance

CHAPTER 4: Better Performance through Antioxidants

Change your nutritional lifestyle now to get long term results and faster recovery times

CHAPTER 5: You Are What You Eat

Commit to improving your mind and body

CHAPTER 6: The Secret to Having the Best Abs Ever

Get the look you want

ABOUT THE AUTHOR

As a certified sports nutritionist and professional athlete, I traveled around the world and competed against some in the world. Being able to share what I have learned and believe in is important to me. My knowledge and experience has helped my students throughout the years. The more you know about the game, the better you will do. Being successful in wrestling requires you to have a strong cardiovascular base because of all the pushing, turning, and pulling that's done.

In wrestling you need to have speed, strength, endurance, flexibility, and agility to win. Nutrition is a key part in the process of winning and that's what this book is all about.

WHY THIS NUTRITION GUIDE?

As a sports nutritionist and professional athlete, I have studied and researched many books on nutrition and diets to help me reach my potential in competition but have noticed that many of the books researched offer solutions through supplements and muscle enhancing formulas which is not what this book is about. If you want a short term and easy solution to nutrition this is not the right book for you? This book is for people who want long lasting and effective results in a natural way that won't cause side effects or problems years later. Yes, you can take supplements and performance enhancing substances if you choose to but they were not created naturally and therefor are not perfect for your body. There are natural ways to feed your body and get great results without future disappointments health wise. I want the best nutrition for my body and you should too. After traveling and finding my favorite nutritional environment in a small village in South America, I decided to adopt their diet and modify it to my athletic needs. That is what you are getting in this book.

Few diet books focus on a real population that has used these nutritional methods for hundreds of years. All athletes should take advantage of this knowledge that has had long lasting success.

For a group of people to live to more than a hundred years of age still vibrant and athletic, as the people of Vilcabamba do, and not have serious health problems, is an astonishing accomplishment. That's why a lot of the research of this book was based on their view of nutrition. Lifestyles based on eating fresh and moderated food servings and consistent DAILY exercise will help you achieve a better lifestyle for years to come.

The following pages will help you realize how easy it could be to follow this nutritional guide and increase your RMR. Combined with regular and daily exercise to build more muscle you will notice the effects on your health; resulting in clearer skin, a more regular digestive system, prevention of multiple illnesses and diseases including hypertension, diabetes, colon cancer, and many others. Also, it may be possible to see improvements in already present illnesses, causing a reduction in the dosage or quantity of current medications by simply eating healthier and exercising regularly.

Let's face it; we all want to live longer but we also want to continue to be productive in our later years! Therefore doesn't it make sense to assimilate what a small village located in a low oxygen, health care deprived, fast food deficient environment has done for hundreds of years with outstanding results? Good luck and have fun changing your lives for the better!

This book and its exercises are the key to helping you achieve your goals. Joseph Correa, a certified sports nutritionist and a professional athlete who has dedicated himself to improving his performance through better nutrition and quality training exercises. Through their extensive knowledge and experience, they are convinced of the importance of proper nutrition and exercise.

This book was created as a step by step and easy to follow guide to getting in shape. To get the most out of it follow these simple steps:

First, read each chapter in order. Don't skip any chapters as you might miss out on important tips that can maximize the benefits to your health.

Second, write down your daily and monthly diet goals based on guidelines provided in this book.

Reread this book once you are done reading the book to reinforce and memorize the valuable topics you will find inside.

Fourth, TAKE THIS BOOK EVERYWHERE YOU GO SO THAT YOU HAVE IT HANDY WHEN YOU WORK OUT OR AS A QUICK REFERENCE.

INTRODUCTION

The Ultimate Guide to Wrestling Nutrition will teach you how to increase your RMR (resting metabolic rate) to accelerate your metabolism and help you change your body for good. Learn how to get in top shape and reach your ideal weight through smart nutrition so that you can perform at your very best. Eating complex carbohydrates, protein, and natural fats in the right amount and percentages as well as increasing your RMR will make you faster, more agile, and more resistant.

This book will help you to:

-Prevent getting cramps.

-Get injured less often.

-Recover faster after competing or training.

-Have more energy before, during, and after competition.

By eating right and improving the way you feed your body you will also reduce injuries and be less prone to them in the future. Being too thick or too thin are two common reasons injuries happen and is the main reason most athletes have trouble reaching their peak performance. Three nutrition plan options are explained in detail. You can choose which one is best for you depending on your overall physical condition. One of the first changes most people who start this nutrition plan see is endurance. They get less tired and have more energy. Any athlete who wants to be in the best shape ever needs to read this book and start making long term changes that will get them where they want to be. No matter where you are right now or what you're doing, you can always improve yourself. EAT RIGHT TO WIN MORE!

Joseph Correa is a certified sports nutritionist and a professional athlete.

MOTIVATION BY NECESSITY

I have a theory that most of the things in life that are important to our development as human beings; we do out of necessity, not because we want to (at least for most of us). For example, cavemen and women had no choice; if they wanted to eat they hunted or grew food with what was available.

We feel the need to be healthy. We feel the need to look better. We feel the need to live longer and in the best physical shape possible. Those are all needs that we feel because it is in our nature to do so.

Having the motivation to take a step forward every day towards these goals is what really matters. Getting up every day and being happy about yourself and what you are accomplishing fuels that motivation dragon in you. I like to call it the "motivation dragon" because you have to feel the fire inside you that in turn will drive you to start and continue with something great. This will ultimately change your life forever.

A change in lifestyle is important but a change in habits is even more critical as this ultimately makes the difference. <u>Habits are unconscious actions that begin as conscious decisions</u>. In other words, you have to decide mentally to do it and then start taking the necessary steps to make it happen so that you can begin doing them unconsciously all the time.

Remind yourself that YOU CAN and YOU WILL REACH YOUR GOALS!

It is my sincere intention to help you get in the best physical shape possible and for you to be happy with the results.

Let's get started with the good stuff!

Disclaimer: Consult with your doctor before starting this nutrition plan. Also, make sure that the nutritional and diet information in this book is reviewed by your doctor before starting or applying them in your life. Take this book when you see your doctor so that he or she can confirm that exercise and diet are right for you.

CHAPTER 1

THE ULTIMATE GUIDE TO WRESTLING NUTRITION:

Maximize Your Potential

Wrestlers require lots of energy to last the entire competition or training and allow them to remain alert for long periods of time without getting tired. This nutrition plan will help you reach this and many of your nutrition goals so that you can get the most out of your body. This nutrition guide closely resembles the eating habits of the people of Vilcabamba who have a record in longevity which serves as a perfect base for any athlete who wants to reach peak performance for the long term and be able to maintain it over the years. They set a great example for all athletes because of their focus on organic energy sources. This will allow all athletes to perform their very best for the longest period of time without any future negative effects on the brain and body unlike some enhanced performance substances that will strip the body of the essential elements to create natural processes in the body and alter them to create short term improvements.

All athletes should eat a lot of fruit, vegetables, and protein derived foods (chicken, eggs, turkey, fish, etc.). Complex carbohydrates intake should be cut down to a maximum of brown rice, pasta, all natural bread, and organic ingredients. In the village of Vilcabamba, they drink mostly water, natural fruit juices, and milk. Everything they eat and drink is composed of natural, non-processed, non-canned, and non-preservative containing foods. Even though some sodas and junk food are sold in the village, these are not suggested in this diet. By using this knowledge about their eating habits and other medical facts, we have created a nutrition guide that will help you to live and compete healthier and to live longer. It will also allow you to control your weight and the shape of your body better.

This is not your typical diet book where you're told about a magical drink that makes you lose weight or pills that make you lose 10 pounds in a week. There are also diets that focus on not eating almost anything at all. Many of these diets have a negative long term effect on your mind and body. <u>The truth is there is NO magic formula!</u> The key to getting in better shape is simply eating right and exercising. Doing those two things the right way is what this book is about.

Why are we focusing on the answer to your problems first?

Knowing what needs to be done does not guarantee that you'll know what steps need to be taken to get there!

Why do we have such a serious obesity and malnutrition problem around the world and why has it become with the youngsters as well?

There's always something in life that you end up neglecting and later regretting. This is specifically true with health. Usually, physical problems start small and then go on to become very difficult to manage and that's why we need to prevent them starting with our youth.

Getting Some Perspective

I try to think of life in very basic terms. If you leave out all of the technological advances that clutter our lives and focus on a more basic lifestyle you will find yourself in a very different environment. What do I mean by this? *Well, let's say we didn't have TV, internet, or cell phones. Let's say there are no cars, planes or escalators. No more hot dogs, hamburgers, soft drinks, and junk food (these are not technological advances but we'll throw them in as well)*. Please don't faint! I know most of us can't live without many of these things but we are just trying to put things into perspective. What have you got left in terms of food? We will still have fruits and vegetables that come from plants and trees. We still have meat in the form of chicken, beef, fish, and pork. But guess what? We may have to hunt for fish or other animals we want to eat and that involves doing physical exercise. We have to walk, climb, and stretch to pick mangoes or apples off trees. All this requires that we walk, run, or otherwise burn more calories.

Now, once we catch or harvest our food we have to prepare it. Do we have a microwave or oven to cook the food? No, but we may have a pan or pot to heat with fire. You might also catch some sun while hunting and picking fruits. Do you know how important a little sun can be to your health? Let's use an example.

In tropical waters, in some parts of the world, pink dolphins exist. As strange as this may sound there is a very logical explanation. These dolphins live in areas of high density of tropical plant life where very little sunlight comes through into the water.

Because of this deficiency in sunlight, their skin has become almost transparent and that gives dolphins a pinkish appearance. You have to see it to believe it, but the point is that you need a little sun as well, so try to get some sun every once in a while. Don't overdo it! Just enough sun is good enough.

I know this is an unusual way of thinking but at least now we know how simple we can make our daily lives while becoming healthier. I am not saying you should live like this, but, you should try to apply some of these basic ideas that have been forgotten due to changes in our society and technological advances. You might decide to walk to the grocery store to buy food and get a workout while doing so. You might decide to park a little further away at work so that you have to do some extra walking. When you're at the park with your kids, jog with them or go swimming over the weekend as a family. Instead of preparing food or eating food prepared with a lot of oil or butter, try boiling it, using the oven, or steam cooking.

Do your best to make sure that the majority of what you eat has a strong nutritional value and is as fresh as possible. This will help you stay healthy and fit, for years to come.

This book is divided into 3 wrestling lifestyles:

Low Cardio Lifestyle Athlete (LCLA):

This dietary phase is for athletes who require less food containing complex carbohydrates (these include but are not limited to: pasta, brown rice, oatmeal, brown beans, lentils, etc.). These people do not need to store up that many energy reserves and therefore should have a higher percentage of foods containing proteins, legumes, vegetables, dairies fruits and other.

LCLA is for athletes who don't do more than 30 minutes of cardio per day as part of their training and also during competition. You can be flexible during competition since some conditions and environmental changes might change just how you can absorb food. This could be because of the country you are competing in, or you might feel nauseous before competing, or it can also be because of the food available in that area.

After the first month of completing this diet phase and complementing it in combination with your regular physical training regiment, you can decide to continue or adapt the diet to your needs in case you feel you need to add more protein or carbs or dairies.

Medium Cardio Lifestyle Athlete (MCLA):

This dietary phase is for athletes who require a specific percentage of foods containing complex carbohydrates (these include but are not limited to: pasta, brown rice, oatmeal, brown beans, lentils, etc.) to maintain a medium cardio-intensive lifestyle, while at the same time consuming a higher percentage of foods containing proteins, dairies, legumes, and fruits.

MCLA is for athletes who complete a minimum of 30 minutes of cardiovascular workouts as part of their daily physical training which may include (if you cross-train): swimming, walking, running, bicycling, jumping, rowing or playing sports that combine any of the aforementioned activities.

High Cardio Lifestyle Athlete (HCLA):

This dietary phase is for athletes who require a larger percentage of foods containing complex carbs to maintain their cardio intensive lifestyles in a balanced and healthy manner, while still maintaining a high percentage of foods containing protein, legumes, vegetables, fruits, and nuts.

HCLA is for people who train more than an hour of daily cardiovascular exercise. At least one hour of high intensity cardio workouts include (if you cross-train): running, swimming, rowing, jumping, or bicycling. This is especially important for athletes who do a lot of cardiovascular exercise as they require more carbohydrates to stay in good physical shape and to allow their bodies to recover.

The USDA Food guide pyramid contains the following groups of food.

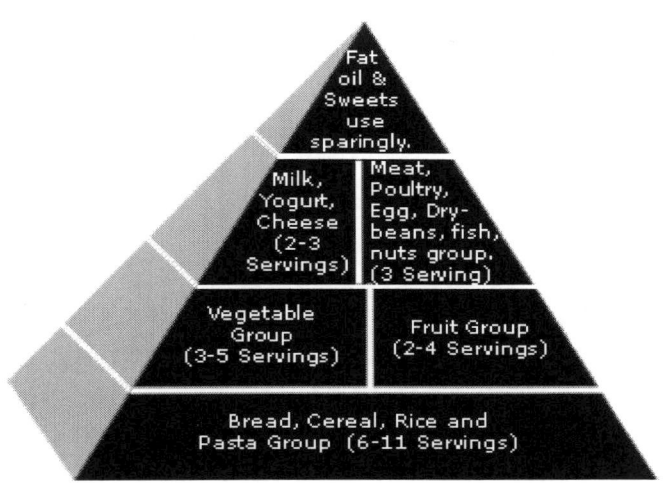

a) Bread, Cereals, Rice, Pasta Group (6 to 11 servings): This group consists of the carbohydrate heavy foods and is placed at the bottom of the pyramid indicating that they should be eaten more often and should form an important part of the daily diet. The rationale behind eating more carbohydrates is that they provide energy so that a person is required to eat less fat. It is recommended that a person should have 6-11 servings from this group.

b) Vegetables (3-5 servings) and Fruit (2-4 servings): There is no doubt that fruit and vegetables are good for the body. Fruit and vegetables provide the body with essential vitamins and other nutrients and ward off diseases and ailments. A person should have 3-5 servings of vegetables and 2-4 servings of fruit a day.

c) Meat, Poultry, Fish, Dry Beans, Eggs and Nuts Group (2-3 servings): This group provides the body with proteins. Proteins help in building the body tissues and muscles. A person should eat 2-3 servings from this group a day.

d) Milk, Yogurt and Cheese Group (2-3 servings): This group provides proteins and calcium that make the bones strong and prevent health problems related to the degeneration of bone mass. A person should eat 2-3 servings from this group a day.

e) Fats, Oils and Sweets (eat sparingly): This group should be eaten sparingly. Fat leads to heart disease and obesity. Too much sugar also leads to obesity which can later create health problems in the future.

The food guide pyramid provides an excellent way to ensure that the body's nutritional requirements are fulfilled properly. By following the guide, an individual will receive all the daily requirements in terms of energy, proteins, vitamins and other essential nutrients.

Here are the recommended sizes of the servings for foods high in carbohydrates.

Vegetables: 1 cup of raw vegetables, or ½ a cup of cooked vegetables, or ¾s of a cup of vegetable juice.
Fruit: 1 medium sized fruit (such as 1 medium sized apple or 1 medium sized orange), ½ a cup of a canned or chopped fruit, or ¾s of a cup of fruit juice.
Bread and cereals: 1 slice of bread; 1 ounce or 2/3 s of a cup of ready-to-eat cereal; ½ a cup of cooked rice, pasta, or cereal; ½ a cup of cooked dry beans, lentils, or dried peas.
Dairy: 1 cup of skimmed or low fat milk.

The proper intake of proteins, fats and carbohydrates for non-athletes is:

Proteins 12%

Carbohydrates 58%

Fats 30%

The proper intake of proteins, fats and carbohydrates for most wrestlers is:

Proteins 10-20%

Carbohydrates 50-65%

Fats 10-25%

Body builders eat more proteins to add muscle and bulk, with the proteins accounting for up to 35-40% of the diet for professional body builders.

Aerobic vs Anaerobic Physical Activity:

There are 2 main types of physical activity: Aerobic activity and anaerobic activity.

Anaerobic activity is defined as the activity undertaken without the presence of oxygen which cannot be sustained for long periods of time. This type of activity relies heavily on the fast twitch muscle fibers. Examples of anaerobic activity are weight lifting and sprinting. Such activities cannot be undertaken for long periods of time. This type of activity helps in building lean tissue and improves the body composition. The anaerobic capacity test is a test that measures the ability of the body to undertake exercise of a short duration and of a very high intensity. The Wingate cycle test is commonly used to test anaerobic capacity.

Aerobic Fitness, also known as cardiovascular fitness is the ability of the body to perform an exercise over an extended period of time in the presence of oxygen. This type of activity relies heavily on slow twitch muscle fibers and includes activities such as cycling and marathon running.

A training program which combines cardiovascular fitness and muscular fitness allows more oxygenated blood to be delivered per beat and increases the myoglobin in the muscles so that they can take up more amounts of oxygen, thus allowing more work to be done. This is why it is a smart decision to cross train. In wrestling, being able to combine both aerobic with anaerobic training will give you the best results before, during, and after competition.

SOME OF THE FOODS THAT ARE TO BE USED FOR NUTRITION PLAN ARE:

Complex Carbohydrates

(Each portion is considered 1 serving)

Morning Carbs (1 cup)

Oatmeal

2 slices of toast

Raisin bran cereal

Oat bran cereal

Whole-wheat cereal

Half a wheat bagel

Half a slice pita bread

1 bran muffin

1 wheat waffle

1 wheat pancake

Mid-day Carbs (1/2 cup)

Brown rice

Pasta

1 slice of wheat toast

Wheat pasta

Wild rice

1 sweet potato

1 baked potato

Black, Kidney and Red beans

Lentils

Peas

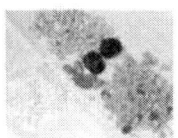   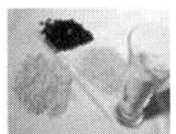

Proteins

(Each portion is considered 1 serving)

No more than 3 dark meats per week and a minimum of 3 types of fish per week.

Morning Proteins	Mid-day proteins	Afternoon Proteins
4 egg whites	4 egg whites	Salmon 4 oz.
Ham 4 oz.	Ham 4 oz.	Ham 4 oz.
Fish (any) 4 oz.	Fish (any) 4 oz.	Fish (any) 4 oz.
1 can of tuna	1 can of tuna	1 can of tuna
Slices of turkey 4oz.	Turkey 4 oz.	Turkey 4 oz
1 cup of shrimp	1 cup of shrimp	Tilapia 4 oz.
Steak or red meat 4 oz.	Steak or red meat 4 oz.	Steak or red meat 2 oz.
1 strip of bacon	Pork 4 oz.	Pork 2 oz.
Chicken or other poultry 4 oz.	Chicken or other poultry 4 oz	Chicken or other poultry 4 oz.

  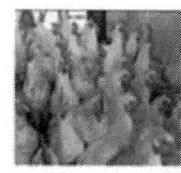 

Seafood (Nutritional Facts)

Cooked (by moist or dry heat with no added ingredients), edible weight portion.
Percent Daily Values (%DV) are based on a 2,000 calorie diet.

Seafood Serving Size (84 g/3 oz)	Calories	Calories from Fat	Total Fat (g)	(%DV)	Saturated Fat (g)	(%DV)	Cholesterol (mg)	(%DV)	Sodium (mg)	(%DV)	Potassium (mg)	(%DV)	Total Carbohydrate (g)	(%DV)	Protein (g)	Vitamin A (%DV)	Vitamin C (%DV)	Calcium (%DV)	Iron (%DV)
Blue Crab	100	10	1	2	0	0	95	32	330	14	300	9	0	0	20	0	4	10	4
Catfish	130	60	6	9	2	10	50	17	40	2	230	7	0	0	17	0	0	0	0
Clams, about 12 small	110	15	1.5	2	0	0	80	27	95	4	470	13	6	2	17	10	0	8	30
Cod	90	5	1	2	0	0	50	17	65	3	460	13	0	0	20	0	2	2	2
Flounder/Sole	100	15	1.5	2	0	0	55	18	100	4	390	11	0	0	19	0	0	2	0
Haddock	100	10	1	2	0	0	70	23	85	4	340	10	0	0	21	2	0	2	6
Halibut	120	15	2	3	0	0	40	13	60	3	500	14	0	0	23	4	0	2	6
Lobster	80	0	0.5	1	0	0	60	20	320	13	300	9	1	0	17	2	0	6	2
Ocean Perch	110	20	2	3	0.5	3	45	15	95	4	290	8	0	0	21	0	2	10	4
Orange Roughy	80	5	1	2	0	0	20	7	70	3	340	10	0	0	16	2	0	4	2
Oysters, about 12 medium	100	35	4	6	1	5	80	27	300	13	220	6	6	2	10	0	6	6	45
Pollock	90	10	1	2	0	0	80	27	110	5	370	11	0	0	20	2	0	0	2
Rainbow Trout	140	50	6	9	2	10	55	18	35	1	370	11	0	0	20	4	4	8	2
Rockfish	110	15	2	3	0	0	40	13	70	3	440	13	0	0	21	4	0	2	2
Salmon, Atlantic/Coho/Sockeye/Chinook	200	90	10	15	2	10	70	23	55	2	430	12	0	0	24	4	4	2	2
Salmon, Chum/Pink	130	40	4	6	1	5	70	23	65	3	420	12	0	0	22	2	0	2	4
Scallops, about 6 large or 14 small	140	10	1	2	0	0	65	22	310	13	430	12	5	2	27	2	0	4	14
Shrimp	100	10	1.5	2	0	0	170	57	240	10	220	6	0	0	21	4	4	6	10

Swordfish	120	50	6	9	1.5	8	40	13	100	4	310	9	0	0	16	2	2	0	6
Tilapia	110	20	2.5	4	1	5	75	25	30	1	360	10	0	0	22	0	2	0	2
Tuna	130	15	1.5	2	0	0	50	17	40	2	480	14	0	0	26	2	2	2	4

Source: U.S. Food and Drug Administration

Vegetables and Legumes

(1-2 cups total of any below)
Vary between raw leafy vegetables, cooked vegetables, and vegetable juice.

Morning V & L's	Mid-day V & L's	Afternoon V & L's
Lettuce	Lettuce	Lettuce
Tomato	Tomato	Tomato
Carrots	Broccoli	Broccoli
Spinach	Carrots	Carrots
Green Peas	Spinach	Spinach
Corn	Green peas	Green peas
Celery	Corn	Corn
Cucumber	Celery	Celery
Vegetable juice	Cucumber	Cucumber
Squash	Vegetable juice	Vegetable juice
String beans	Squash	Squash
Mushrooms	String beans	String beans
Sprouts	Cauliflower	Cauliflower
Beets	Mushrooms	Mushrooms
	Cabbage	Cabbage
	Peppers	Peppers
	Sprouts	Sprouts
	Beets	Beets

Vegetables (*Nutritional Facts*)

Raw, edible weight portion. Percent Daily Values (%DV) are based on a 2,000 calorie diet.

Vegetables Serving Size (gram weight/ ounce weight)	Calories	Calories from Fat	Total Fat (g)	Sodium (mg)	Potassium (mg)	Total Carbohydrates (g)	Dietary Fiber (g)	Sugars (g)	Protein (g)	Vitamin A (%DV)	Vitamin C (%DV)	Calcium (%DV)	Iron (%DV)
Asparagus 5 spears (93 g/3.3 oz)	20	0	0	0	230	4	1	2	2	10	15	2	2
Bell Pepper 1 medium (148 g/5.3 oz)	25	0	0	40	220	6	2	2	1	4	190	2	4
Broccoli 1 medium stalk (148 g/5.3 oz)	45	0	0.5	80	460	8	3	3	4	6	220	6	6
Carrot 1 carrot, 7" long, 1 1/4" diameter (78 g/2.8 oz)	30	0	0	60	250	7	2	2	1	110	10	2	2
Cauliflower 1/6 medium head (99 g/3.5 oz)	25	0	0	30	270	5	2	2	2	0	100	2	2
Celery 2 medium stalks (110 g/3.9 oz)	15	0	0	115	260	4	1	2	0	10	15	4	2
Cucumber 1/3 medium (99 g/3.5 oz)	10	0	0	0	140	2	1	1	1	4	10	2	2
Green (Snap) Beans 3/4 cup cut (83 g/3.0 oz)	20	0	0	0	200	5	3	12	1	4	10	4	2
Green Cabbage 1/12 medium head (84 g/3.0 oz)	25	0	0	20	190	5	2	8	1	0	70	4	2
Green Onion 1/4 cup chopped (25 g/0.9 oz)	10	0	0	10	70	2	1	1	0	2	8	2	2

Vegetable																		
Iceberg Lettuce 1/6 medium head (89 g/3.2 oz)	10	0	0	0	10	0	125	4	2	1	1	4	2	1	6	6	2	2
Leaf Lettuce 1 1/2 cups shredded (85 g/3.0 oz)	15	0	0	0	35	1	170	5	2	1	1	4	1	1	130	6	2	4
Mushrooms 5 medium (84 g/3.0 oz)	20	0	0	0	15	0	300	9	3	1	1	4	0	3	0	2	0	2
Onion 1 medium (148 g/5.3 oz)	45	0	0	0	5	0	190	5	11	4	3	12	9	1	0	20	4	4
Potato 1 medium (148 g/5.3 oz)	110	0	0	0	0	0	620	18	26	9	2	8	1	3	0	45	2	6
Radishes 7 radishes (85 g/3.0 oz)	10	0	0	0	55	2	190	5	3	1	1	4	2	0	0	30	2	2
Summer Squash 1/2 medium (98 g/3.5 oz)	20	0	0	0	0	0	260	7	4	1	2	8	2	1	6	30	2	2
Sweet Corn kernels from 1 medium ear (90 g/3.2 oz)	90	20	2.5	4	0	0	250	7	18	6	2	8	5	4	2	10	0	2
Sweet Potato 1 medium, 5" long, 2" diameter (130 g/4.6 oz)	100	0	0	0	70	3	440	13	23	8	4	16	7	2	120	30	4	4
Tomato 1 medium (148 g/5.3 oz)	25	0	0	0	20	1	340	10	5	2	1	4	3	1	20	40	2	4

Source: U.S. Food and Drug Administration

Fruits, Nuts, and Seeds (*Vary between raw fruit, frozen fruit, fruit juice, and dried fruit.*)

Fruits (1-2 cups)	Nuts (1-2 table spoons)	Seeds/other (1-2 table spoons)
Apples	Peanuts	Sunflower seeds
Pears	Cashews	Dried pumpkin seeds
Bananas	Walnuts	Flax seeds
Pineapple	Pistachio nuts	Sesame Seeds
Oranges	Almonds	Avocado
Tangerines	Hazelnuts	Black olives
Grapefruit	Brazilian nuts	Green olives
Blackberries	Pecans	Flaxseed oil
Blueberries	Macadamia nuts	Canola oil
Strawberries		Olive oil
Plums		
Peaches		
Cherries		
Passion fruit		
Papaya		
Kiwi		
Cantaloupe		
Watermelon		
Fruit juice		

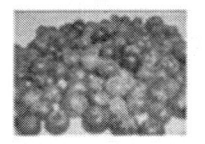

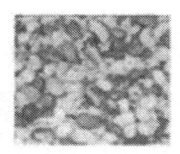

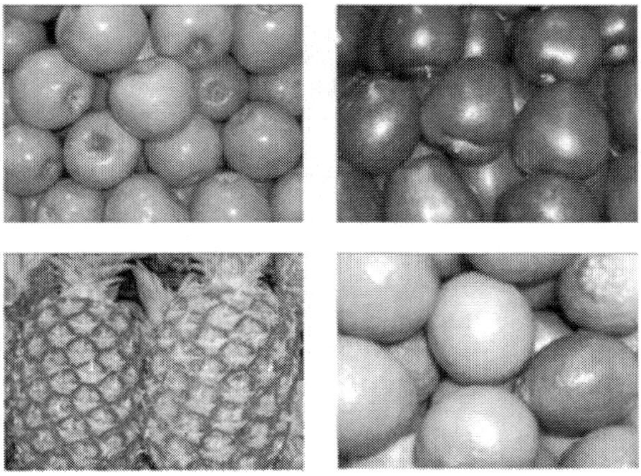

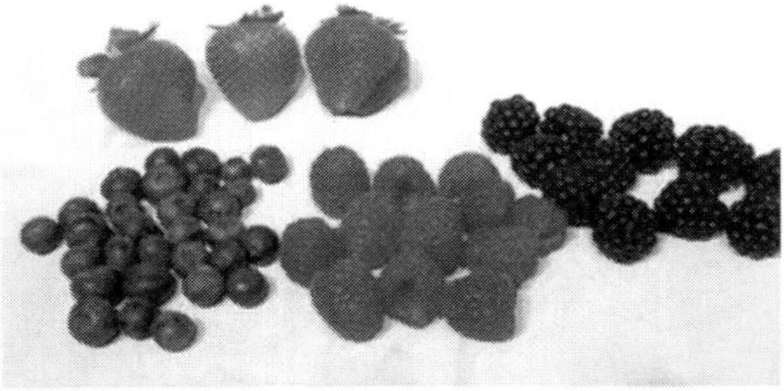

Fruits (*Nutritional Facts*)

Raw, edible weight portion. Percent Daily Values (%DV) are based on a 2,000 calorie diet.

Fruits Serving Size (gram weight/ ounce weight)	Calories	Calories from Fat	Total Fat (g)	(%DV)	Sodium (mg)	(%DV)	Potassium (mg)	(%DV)	Total Carbohydrate (g)	(%DV)	Dietary Fiber (g)	(%DV)	Sugars (g)	Protein (g)	Vitamin A (%DV)	Vitamin C (%DV)	Calcium (%DV)	Iron (%DV)
Apple 1 large (242 g/8 oz)	130	0	0	0	0	0	260	7	34	11	5	20	25	1	2	8	2	2
Avocado California, 1/5 medium (30 g/1.1 oz)	50	35	4.5	7	0	0	140	4	3	1	1	4	0	1	0	4	0	2
Banana 1 medium (126 g/4.5 oz)	110	0	0	0	0	0	450	13	30	10	3	12	19	1	2	15	0	2
Cantaloupe 1/4 medium (134 g/4.8 oz)	50	0	0	0	20	1	240	7	12	4	1	4	11	1	120	80	2	2
Grapefruit 1/2 medium (154 g/5.5 oz)	60	0	0	0	0	0	160	5	15	5	2	8	11	1	35	100	4	0
Grapes 3/4 cup (126 g/4.5 oz)	90	0	0	0	15	1	240	7	23	8	1	4	20	0	0	2	2	0
Honeydew-Melon 1/10 medium melon (134 g/4.8 oz)	50	0	0	0	30	1	210	6	12	4	1	4	11	1	2	45	2	2
Kiwifruit 2 medium (148 g/5.3 oz)	90	10	1	2	0	0	450	13	20	7	4	16	13	1	2	240	4	2
Lemon 1 medium (58 g/2.1 oz)	15	0	0	0	0	0	75	2	5	2	2	8	2	0	0	40	2	0
Lime 1 medium (67 g/2.4 oz)	20	0	0	0	0	0	75	2	7	2	2	8	0	0	0	35	0	0

Food	Cal																	
Nectarine, 1 medium (140 g/5.0 oz)	60	5	0.5	1	0	0	250	7	15	5	2	8	11	1	8	15	0	2
Orange, 1 medium (154 g/5.5 oz)	80	0	0	0	0	0	250	7	19	6	3	12	14	1	2	130	6	0
Peach, 1 medium (147 g/5.3 oz)	60	0	0.5	1	0	0	230	7	15	5	2	8	13	1	6	15	0	2
Pear, 1 medium (166 g/5.9 oz)	100	0	0	0	0	0	190	5	26	9	6	24	16	1	0	10	2	0
Pineapple, 2 slices, 3" diameter, 3/4" thick (112 g/4 oz)	50	0	0	0	10	0	120	3	13	4	1	4	10	1	2	50	2	2
Plums, 2 medium (151 g/5.4 oz)	70	0	0	0	0	0	230	7	19	6	2	8	16	1	8	10	0	2
Strawberries, 8 medium (147 g/5.3 oz)	50	0	0	0	0	0	170	5	11	4	2	8	8	1	0	160	2	2
Sweet Cherries, 21 cherries; 1 cup (140 g/5.0 oz)	100	0	0	0	0	0	350	10	26	9	1	4	16	1	2	15	2	2
Tangerine, 1 medium (109 g/3.9 oz)	50	0	0	0	0	0	160	5	13	4	2	8	9	1	6	45	4	0
Watermelon, 1/18 medium melon; 2 cups diced pieces (280 g/10.0 oz)	80	0	0	0	0	0	270	8	21	7	1	4	20	1	30	25	2	4

Dairy Foods and Snacks *(Each is 1 serving)*
Preferably low-fat dairies

(Each is 1 serving)

Preferably low-fat dairies

Dairy Foods   Snacks

1 cup of milk (8 oz.)   1 fruit bar

1 cup of soy milk (8 oz.)   Dried fruit (1/2 cup)

Low fat cheese (2 slices)   Dark chocolate (1 table spoon)

½ cup cottage cheese   1 multigrain bar

1 cup low fat yogurt (8 oz.)   5 low salt crackers

¼ cup low fat mozzarella cheese   1 protein bar

¼ cup soy cheese   Pretzels (1/2 cup)

1 low fat ice cream yogurt bar   Popcorn (1/2 cup)

1 cup low fat fruit yogurt (8 oz.)   1 low-fat rice cake

HELPFUL TIPS:

- Keep any condiments in your food to a minimum of one teaspoon per meal. Just enough to give your food some flavor.
- Instead of sugar, use honey to sweeten your drinks and food. If you absolutely have to use sugar make sure it's brown sugar.

Sports nutrition is more than just what you eat;

It's when and how you eat!

Drink at least 6-8 glasses of water per day

Drink 1 glass of water when you wake up, 1 before every meal, and 1 before going to sleep.

Eat 6 small to medium size meals per day

You should be eating every three hours. Use a timer, a stop watch or your cell phone to keep track of time as this is just as important as what you eat. If you eat small to medium size meals every three hours, you allow your body to digest food in an efficient manner and in a way that does not overwork the digestive system. Some people eat three large meals a day and then have to wait several hours until they don't feel full again but this is exactly what not to do.

Chew then swallow!

Sounds simple enough, but with today's busy schedules people tend to skip chewing and go directly to swallowing. That won't allow your body to process food the way it should, so make sure you take the time to chew your food. Your teeth have a purpose and that purpose is to break down food before it gets to your stomach so that it may do what it was intended to do. Remember, not chewing your food means your stomach has to work harder and that equates to a longer wait time for digestion that may cause you discomfort or gas.

No carbs or fruit after sunset

There's no need to store up energy you're not going to use while you sleep. Try to stay away from large meals after sunset. Be sure to consume a healthy snack if need be to prevent yourself from overeating during those times or simply drink a glass of water.

Always find time to exercise or do some form of stretching when you wake up, as this is the ideal time of day to get in shape and stay injury free.

Nutritional Guide for L C L A's

Monday – Saturday (daily percentage to be consumed)

20% complex carbs – 20% proteins – 30% vegetables and legumes –

15% fruits and nuts – 15% dairy foods and snacks

Or the equivalent in daily servings

Carbs (1-2 servings) – proteins (3-4 servings) – vegetables and legumes (3-6

servings) – Fruits and nuts (1.5-3 servings) – dairy foods and

snacks (1.5 servings)

Sunday

(Some athletes don't train on Sundays or once a week so one day per week the food servings will change. We are using Sunday as that day.)

15% carbs – 25% proteins – 20% vegetables and legumes –

20% fruits and nuts – 20% dairy foods and snacks

Or the equivalent in servings

Carbs (1.5-3 servings) – proteins (2.5-3 servings) – vegetables and legumes (2

servings) – Fruits and nuts (2-3 servings) – dairy foods and

snacks (2 servings)

The percentages shown are for the daily consumption of these food groups and the servings are for the maximum amount of times you are allowed to consume these food groups. Follow the food group charts provided at the beginning of the book as a guide to what you can eat except for the dairies which you are free to choose the type and amount due to the variety of preferences and medical conditions out there.

Nutritional Guide for M C L A's

Monday - Saturday

15% carbs – 30% proteins – 25% vegetables and legumes –

15% fruits and nuts – 15% dairy foods and snacks

Or the equivalent in daily servings

Carbs (1.5-3 servings) – proteins (3-6 servings) – vegetables and legumes (2.5-6 servings) – Fruits and nuts (1.5-3 servings) – dairy foods and

snacks (1.5-3 servings)

Sunday

(Some athletes don't train on Sundays or once a week so one day per week the food servings will change. We are using Sunday as that day.)

25% carbs – 20 % proteins – 20% vegetables and legumes –

20% fruits and nuts – 15% dairy foods and snacks

Or the equivalent in servings

Carbs (2.5-3 servings) – proteins (2-5 servings) – vegetables and legumes (2

servings) – Fruits and nuts (2 servings) – dairy foods and

snacks (1.5 servings)

*The percentages shown are for the daily consumption of these food groups and the servings are for the maximum amount of times you are allowed to consume these food groups. Follow the food group charts provided at the beginning of the book as a guide to what you can eat except for the dairies which you are free to choose the type and amount due to the variety of preferences and medical conditions out there.

Nutritional Guide for H C L A's

Monday - Saturday

20% carbs – 25% proteins – 20% vegetables and legumes –

15% fruits and nuts – 20% dairy foods and snacks

Or the equivalent in daily servings

Carbs (2 servings) – proteins (2.5 servings) – vegetables and legumes (2 servings) – Fruits and nuts (1.5 servings) – dairy foods and snacks (2 servings)

Sunday

(Some athletes don't train on Sundays or once a week so one day per week the food servings will change. We are using Sunday as that day.)

25% carbs – 20% proteins – 15% vegetables and legumes –

20% fruits and nuts – 20% dairy foods and snacks

Or the equivalent in servings

Carbs (2.5 servings) – proteins (2 servings) – vegetables and legumes (1.5

servings) – Fruits and nuts (2 servings) – dairy foods and

snacks (2 servings)

The percentages shown are for the daily consumption of these food groups and the servings are for the maximum amount of times you are allowed to consume these food groups. Follow the food group charts provided at the beginning of the book as a guide to what you can eat except for the dairies which you are free to choose the type and amount due to the variety of preferences and medical conditions out there.

CHAPTER 2

EAT, SLEEP, AND BREATHE YOUR WAY TO A LEANER BODY

Your Secret Weapon RMR

RMR is also known as resting metabolic rate and is the number of calories burned while your body is at rest because of normal body functions such as the heart rate and the breathing function. This accounts for 75% of the total calories burned during the day. This can vary from one person to another depending on age, amount of fat in your body, and other factors. The less fat you have in your body and the more muscle you have the higher the RMR will be and the faster you will burn calories at rest, even in your sleep. This is what some people consider as having a good metabolism but it really equates to having a high RMR. Having a high RMR will make you leaner and make easier for you to stay leaner every day. How to do you accomplish this? You can do this by changing what you eat to reduce fats and sugars, and by adding muscle to your body.

Each and every day is an opportunity to get back in shape. When you're tired of work and constantly busy with all the tedious things in life, you stop thinking about the importance of taking care of your body and mind. For this reason, I have prepared a daily schedule to help you <u>get in shape all day even while you eat, sleep, and breathe.</u> How is this possible? You can do this by simply by accelerating your metabolism. A natural way of doing this is by making small changes in your life that have an immediate effect on your body.

This daily schedule can be changed to accommodate your lifestyle as well as your training schedule. <u>Things you already do on a normal day will be highlighted in bold just to</u>

remind you that you're not really changing your day to day schedule at all.

Remember, you are the only one that can keep yourself motivated enough to go through with the schedule. Working out every day and sticking to this nutrition guide requires sacrifice and being able to let go of temptations.

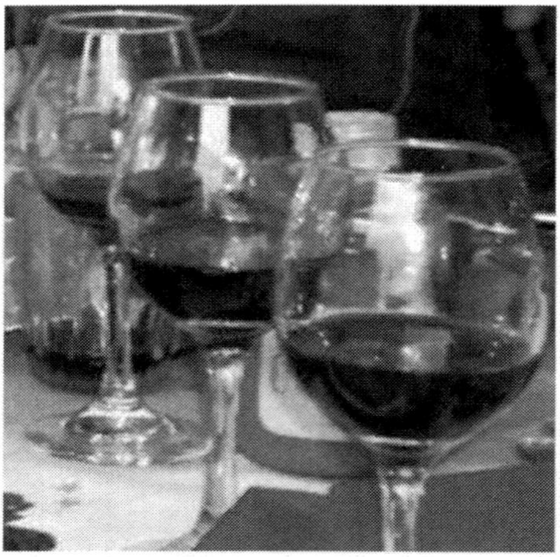

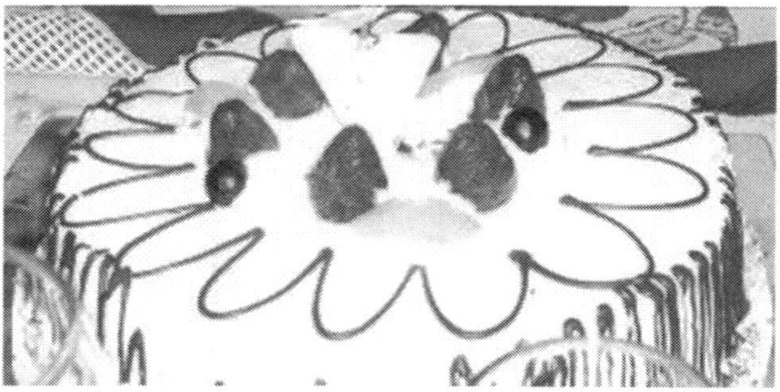

Temptations

Every day we pass by a pastry shop or a vending machine full of goodies. These are the moments you have to stay strong. Look away! Think of something else. Think of work. Think of your family. Think of how hard you're working to get and stay in shape. There's no one to stop you from eating a donut or a soft drink or potato chips, it's up to you to be disciplined. Every time you're able to withstand temptation, you'll be that much stronger. In case you've never done this before, don't go to the grocery store on an empty stomach as you will definitely buy things you should not be eating.

Stop smoking

Smoking WILL lower your life expectancy and more importantly it WILL decrease your quality of life! This nutrition guide should be used to improve your longevity and performance as an athlete through physical exercise and improved nutrition. Smoking will work against you and your goals to improve your health habits.

Consume less alcohol

Drinking alcohol will dehydrate you much faster than most any other drinks so it would not be recommended you add this to your nutrition plan. Consult with your doctor to find out just how much is enough for you.

Improving your breathing techniques

Static breathing exercises, Yoga, Pilates, stretching, and other forms of breathing exercises will help you reduce your stress levels.

Less stress = A longer life

These exercises are for both men and women. They have changed my life and I am sure they will do the same for you. These are just some of the benefits you will see:

- Increased flexibility
- Stronger back and core muscles
- Improved posture
- Reduced stress

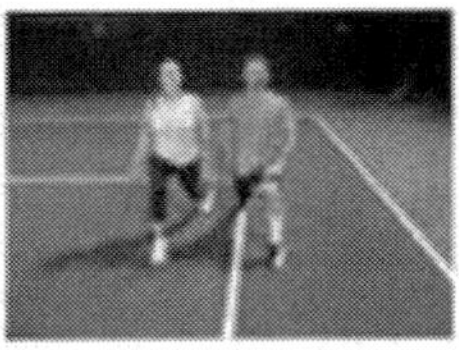

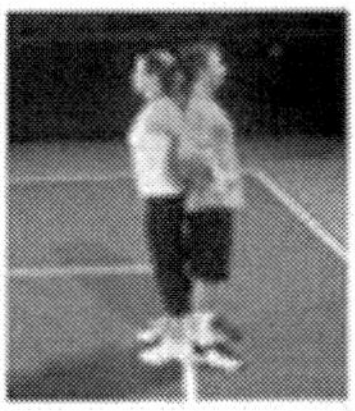

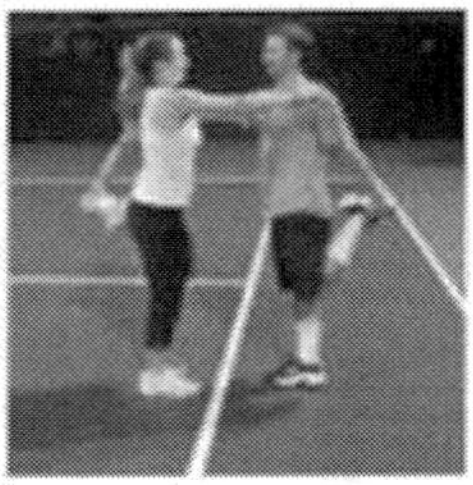

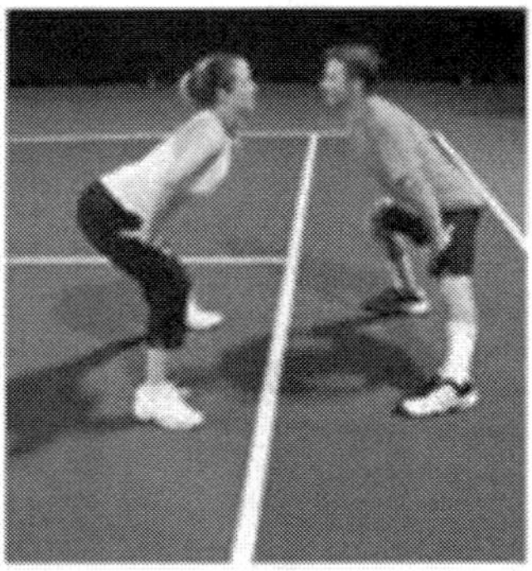

The Ideal Nutrition and Workout Schedule

Monday - Friday

7:00 AM	Drink one glass of water when you *wake up*.
7:15 AM	Complete a minimum of 5 abdominal exercises or 5 stretching exercises.
8:00 AM	Drink a glass of water, milk, or juice and then *eat breakfast*. Base your breakfast on the diet plan explained in chapter 1.
8:30 AM	Train as you normally would on a weekday.
10:00 AM	Drink one glass of water.
11:00 AM	Eat a fruit along with a multigrain bar (or another

	snack based on the list provided in chapter 1.). You can add or replace it with a yogurt or slices of a protein (turkey, ham, roast beef, fish, poultry, etc.).
11:10 AM	After having your snack make sure to take a 5 minute break to stretch and breathe, or simply relax your body so that you prepare your body for lunch in a peaceful environment.
2:00 PM	Drink a glass of water, juice, milk or other liquid and then *have lunch*.
2:45 PM	Rest at least 30 minutes to 1 hour to allow your body to fully digest the food.

4:00 PM	Start your afternoon training which might include going to the gym or simply resting if your morning training was enough.
5:00 PM	Complete the abdominal exercises provided in chapter 6.
6:30 PM	Drink a glass of water, milk, or juice before *having dinner*. Remember to eat only foods explained in the nutrition plan in the first chapter.
8:30 PM	Eat a snack if your still hungry. Make sure to eat small quantities. <u>Remember that after dark you do not eat any carbs, fruits or foods that contain either one.</u>

10:00 PM   *You should drink at least one glass of water before going to sleep even if you sleep earlier or later than the time provided.*

Note:

You can adjust the schedule and the exercises as long as all the steps are completed and are in order. Also, make sure you stay within the 3 hour time difference between meals and drink a minimum of 6 – 8 glasses of water before the end of the day.

Improving the quality of events in your life and daily schedule will help you lose weight even while you are sleeping as your metabolism will accelerate at a faster rate and will move its way to your sleeping hours.

Saturday

For Saturday's schedule we are simply going to replace the time at work with time at home, entertainment, or doing some chores. Saturday would look something like this:

7:00 AM	Drink one glass of water when you *wake up*.

7:15 AM	Do a 5 minute morning stretch to get your muscles relaxed and ready for the day ahead.

8:00 AM	Drink a glass of water, milk, or juice and then *eat breakfast*. Base your breakfast on the diet plan explained in chapter 1.

8:30 AM	Train as you normally would on a weekday.

10:00 AM	Drink one glass of water.

11:00 AM	Eat a fruit along with a multigrain bar (or another snack based on the list provided in chapter 1.). You can add or replace it with a yogurt or slices of a protein (turkey, ham, roast beef, fish, poultry, etc.).
11:10 AM	After having your snack make sure to take a 5 minute break to stretch and breathe, or simply relax your body so that you prepare your body for lunch in a peaceful environment.
2:00 PM	Drink a glass of water, juice, milk or other liquid and then *have lunch*.
2:45 PM	Rest

5:30 PM		Drink a glass of water, milk, or juice before *having dinner*. Remember to eat only foods in the nutrition guide provided at the beginning of this book.

8:30 PM		Eat a small meal and include a glass of water with this meal.

10:00 PM	Drink a glass of water before going to *sleep*.

Your Daily Diet and Exercise Log

Make sure to make copies for every day you complete this log. Save all completed logs so that you can review them at the end of the month. Use the schedule below as a reference for completing this log.

TIME	MY DIET AND EXERCISE ROUTINE FOR TODAY *DIET - EXERCISE - LOCATION*
7:00am	
8:00am	
9:00am	
10:00am	
11:00am	
12:00pm	
1:00pm	
2:00pm	
3:00pm	
4:00pm	
5:00pm	
6:00pm	

7:00pm	
8:00pm	
9:00pm	
10:00pm	

Comments:

CHAPTER 3

HOW TO GET IN SHAPE

24 HOURS A DAY

Accelerating your metabolism to enhance performance

What you do if I told you that you could get in shape 24 hours a day? Sound impossible? Let me tell you how to do it through a very simple process that might surprise you in a sense because of its simplicity but first we will focus on the three main components of staying in shape and losing weight. They are: Patience, repetition, and focus.

Patience

It takes time to gain weight. Some people spend a year or more increasing their weight without ever controlling it. Dropping all that weight that has taken so long to accumulate takes time if you want lasting results. Let me repeat that one more time because it's a difficult concept to understand. It takes time to drop all the weight you have accumulated over the years. If you want quick results just work smarter and improve your nutrition. If you lose weight fast, be sure that it will come back just as fast if you don't continue to do what you did to drop it. *Don't fall for the easy way out* because it won't last and you'll be right back where you started. Be patient as small decreases in weight are more valuable in the long run than large ones that come right back. Your body will gradually adjust to the exercise routines and the nutritional plan. That means you will be building off your new results each time. Just be patient.

BALANCED WEIGHT

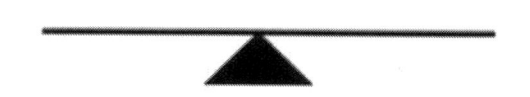

Over time your body weight works like a seesaw.

Your weight will increase as time goes by if you don't take the necessary steps to maintain it at a healthy level and it will decrease as time goes by if you work hard to control it. Maintaining your body weight is a matter of balance between nutrition and exercise (above).

UNBALANCED WEIGHT

Repetition

Changing your lifestyle takes time and it takes permanent decisions. If you decide to start working out but find yourself training once a week or every other week, then you obviously know what type of results you will have. You've got to be consistent. Also, you need to be repetitive in what you, from the first day of the month until the last day of the month. It sounds like a lot of work, but you have to realize that you already do a lot of things in a consistent manner that you might not have noticed. Do you eat at least three times a day, every day of every month of the year? <u>Do you watch TV at least an hour every day of every month?</u> Do you change your clothes every day of every month of the year? And do you take a shower every day of every month of the year? If you answered "yes" to these questions, it means you do a lot of things in a consistent way. I bet a lot of people never even realize they do all these things every day. It's definitely something you should use to your advantage, by simply adding some exercises and an effective diet plan to these everyday activities.

There are "quick fixes" that can get you where you want to be but most of the time they'll have some sort of side effect or health risk involved. That's not what this book is about. You're working on obtaining <u>long term results that will last</u> and that will eventually become a part of your life. That's why it's important to stick to these exercises and allow them to become a part of your daily life.

The most important thing is to be consistent if you want long term results so stay focused on getting there.

Focus

Focus is the art of being able to concentrate on something for a determined period of time. That's what I want you to do with your new exercise routine and dietary plan. Stay focused no matter what. Stay focused on the objective at hand. Stay focused on your new lifestyle. Work at it every day because it's your life and it's up to you and no one else to make it better.

How to get in shape 24 hours a day

We spoke about increasing your RMR in the last chapter but now let's go into more detail.

Step 1: Start doing more exercise, preferably the exercises that involve increasing the amount of muscle in your body. Your body will to have to regenerate muscle tissue during the night time and this will contribute towards burning more energy. By doing this, you will lose weight and get fitter during the entire day!

Step 2: Follow the nutritional instructions described in chapter 1. Eating better and at scheduled times will change the short and long term effects your body and mind will have over time by reducing fat and simple sugar intake. This will help you to have a better defense mechanism that in turn will prevent you from getting sick or injured. It will boost your energy levels as well as help prevent future health problems such as obesity and heart disease. This is just to name a few of the most common ailments affecting our society today.

Step 3: Non-athletes need to drink a minimum of 6 to 8 glasses of water during the day, <u>especially one glass upon waking up and one before going to sleep.</u> As an athlete you should drink 6-10 glasses of water.

The Right Way to Drink Water

Water intake before the exercise, during the exercise and after the exercise should be properly planned.

A) Before training or competition consume 14-18 ounces of water two hours before any exercise. The two hour gap is enough to fully hydrate the body and leave enough time for excess water to come out of the system.

Take 5-7 ounces of water just 15 minutes before training.

B) During training or competition an athlete must constantly keep hydrating the body every 20-25 minutes with 5-10 ounces of water. Sports drinks are good sources of sodium which needs to be replenished in competition but should be mixed with some water to dilute the high sugar content they usually have to make them taste good.

Athletes who perspire excessively should consume 1.5 g of sodium and 2.3 g of chloride each day (or 3.8 g of salt) to replace the amount lost through perspiration. The maximum amount should not exceed 5.8 g of salt each day (2.3 g of sodium). Consult with your doctor if you have any of these medical conditions: elevated blood pressure, coronary heart disease, diabetes, and kidney disease, etc. These athletes should avoid consuming salt at the upper level. Endurance athletes and other individuals who are involved in strenuous activities are allowed to consume more sodium to offset sweat losses. The carbonates in the sports drinks also help the muscles perform better. Athletes should also have an adequate intake of 4.7 g of potassium per day to blunt the effects of salt, lower blood pressure, and reduce the risk of kidney stones and bone loss. Athletes should also eat foods rich in potassium such as bananas and prunes.

C) After training or competition an athlete should replace all lost fluids by drinking approximately 20 ounces of fluid for every pound of weight lost.

Step 4: Sleep at least 5 hours but no more than 10 per day and take power naps during the day if you feel you need to get more rest. Sleeping allows your body to recover from the wear and tear you experience every day. It's also a good time for your body to recover so that you can continue training the following day. Sleeping is an excellent way to relieve your body and mind of any excess stress that has accumulated during the day. Sleeping is important so make sure you get adequate hours of sleep every night.

Step 5: Working your cardiovascular endurance is a great way to accelerate your metabolism which will also strengthen your heart. Make sure you do as much aerobic exercise as possible without getting injured. Besides static exercises and stretching, aerobic exercises will provide you with one of the most important tools you can have towards having a higher resting metabolic rate which we talked about in the last chapter. Some good aerobic exercises you can do to cross train are: running, swimming, jumping, roller-blading, skiing, rowing, karate, and playing sports that require any combination of these. A good cardiovascular exercise you can do after lunch is walk up and down stairs at a slow pace and at a low intensity level. If you work or live in a building that has stairs, make sure you take advantage of this. A building with two floors would be sufficient since you can go up and down the same steps. Make sure you do this for at least 5 minutes to make it worthwhile. After eating, always try to do some form of low-intensity aerobic exercise besides walking up and down stairs. This might be one of the most important changes you make towards improving your overall health and fitness.

Our goal in this chapter is to naturally accelerate your metabolism by staying as active as possible during most of the day which will increase your RMR. A faster metabolism helps your body stay lean and fit but you want to make sure you do this naturally (without the use of artificial substances) and gradually so that these changes are easily maintained in months and years to come.

A SIMPLE EXPLANATION ON LOSING, GAINING, AND MAINTAINING BODY WEIGHT

Losing, gaining, and maintaining weight is all about simple math. If you consume 1 unit of food and exercise 1 unit, you will have a simple mathematical equation that looks like this:

$$1 - 1 = 0$$

Meaning, if you exercise the same amount you eat (unit wise) you should gain little or no weight.

Now, if you consume 1 unit of food and exercise "0" units, you will have an equation that looks like this:

$$1 - 0 = 1$$

Meaning, you will have gained "1" unit of weight. (I use the term "unit" to simplify things but it refers to the amount of weight.) This simply means that every day that you eat and don't exercise, you gain weight because you have a surplus.

Last, if you consume "1" unit of food and exercise "2" units, you will have an equation that will look like this:

$$1 - 2 = -1$$

Meaning, you have lost one unit of weight.

Important note: Not consuming any units of food (not eating) is not an option because this will create more harm than good. Instead of achieving your goals you will be delaying them and even causing irreversible health problems. You need food to survive. It is a basic necessity of life.

WHAT DOES THIS ALL MEAN?

The amount and quality of exercise you do will determine if you lose, gain, or maintain weight. Depending on what your goals are, this can actually make your life healthier. Just make sure to follow a nutritional plan that is right for you and your lifestyle. Refer to chapter 1 for more information on what you should be eating and how much of it. Warning! Do not go to extremes. Some people get sick by going on extreme diets that can ultimately create more harm than benefit. Below are some examples of extremes you want to avoid:

EXAMPLE 1

By eating simple sugars and fats, and NOT consuming food with nutritional value will reduce your potential performance outcome and will lower your quality of health in years to come. A balanced diet is necessary to stay fit. Even though this would not be considered an extreme diet it is still suggested that you stay away from prepackaged and canned foods, as well as foods with high fat content not derived from natural sources. Natural sources of fat would be avocado, nuts, olive oil, etc. and these are good for you but in the right proportions.

EXAMPLE 2

If you are an athlete that does a lot of cardio exercise and don't consume any carbohydrates such as bread, rice, and pasta. It can seriously affect your performance as well as your wellbeing. Cutting carbs completely out of your diet might not be a wise decision. If this is the case, you should consume some form of carbohydrate during the day to maintain the right energy reserves your body needs. You can still control your body weight but you have to consume at least a minimum of nutrients from a variety of food groups and this includes carbohydrates.

EXAMPLE 3

Eating a lot and not exercising. This is what this book focuses on preventing. This book will definitely help you to get fitter and improve the shape of your body into the body you've always wanted as a wrestler. Make it a priority to balance your nutritional life with everyday cardiovascular training.

EXAMPLE 4

Not sleeping enough can severely affect your mental and physical condition during training and competition. Sleeping allows you to recover and perform better in all aspects of your life. Take the necessary steps to control the amount and quality of your sleep.

CHAPTER 4

BETTER PERFORMANCE THROUGH ANTIOXIDANTS

Change your nutritional lifestyle now to get long term results and faster recovery times

A number of elements in our body such as sunlight and pollution in our environment produce oxidation leading to the production of dangerous chemical compounds called free radicals. Free radicals can lead to serious cellular damage, which is the common pathway for cancer, ageing, and a variety of other diseases. Free radicals are highly reactive and pose a major threat by reacting with cell membranes in chain reactions leading to the death of the cells. Antioxidants are molecules that can help in destroying the free radicals so that the body can be free from the dangers associated with the free radicals. Moreover, athletes should have a keen interest in them because of health concerns and the prospect of enhanced performance and/or recovery after exercise. The way antioxidants work is that they can react with the free radicals and shut down the chain reaction leading to the death of the DNA cells and thus save them.

The main sources of antioxidants are:

1. Vitamin E: It is an antioxidant and helps protect cells from damage. It is also important for the health of red blood cells. Vitamin E is found in many foods such as vegetable oils, nuts, and leafy green vegetables. Avocados, wheat germ, and whole grains are also good sources of this vitamin.

2. Beta-carotene: It is a precursor to vitamin A (retinol) and is present in liver, egg yolk, milk, butter, spinach, carrots, tomatoes, and grains.

3. Vitamin C: It is needed to form collagen, a tissue that helps in holding cells together. It is essential for healthy bones, teeth, gums, and blood vessels. It helps the body absorb iron and calcium, aids in wound healing, and contributes to brain function. You will find high levels of vitamin C in red berries, kiwifruit, red and green bell peppers, tomatoes, broccoli, spinach, and juices made from guava, grapefruit, and orange.

4. Selenium: It is a trace element and is also an important antioxidant.

Some Popular Antioxidants are Mentioned Below:

Strengthening our immune system will help you absorb antioxidants and protect you from free radicals which can be done through exercise. That's why a combination of cardiovascular and weight training in combination with added antioxidants in your diet will improve you performance and allow you to have less low energy or sick days. By consuming more antioxidants your recovery phase will be faster which will allow you to compete sooner than normal.

Project the Right Image through a Better Posture to Win More

Studies have shown that athletes who project a strong positive image are prone to being more successful and have a stronger immune system. Having a strong immune system will keep you healthier and prone to less injuries which equates to having the prospect of winning more simply because you can compete more often.

Definitive change from the caveman era to now is our posture. For some reason a lot of athletes look like they are back in the caveman era. Maybe some athletes have this hunched posture because they don't work on flexibility and back strengthening exercises or maybe because of lack of confidence. Whatever may be the reason, an athlete's posture says a lot about how they feel and what they project specially to their competition. Showing a lack of confidence to your competition will only motivate them to do better.

To succeed more as an athlete start showing more confidence through a better posture even when you are not competing.

Most of us forget that as we get older our backs hunch even more and it becomes more difficult to stay straight. I would rather work on having a better posture now than later because later might never come. I forgot to mention that not standing up straight makes you look fatter as well. So if you want to start looking thinner, start standing up straight! For this and many other reasons, it's essential to focus on your posture.

It has often been overlooked by many but can help you get to a better figure faster than you can imagine. Did you know that by walking in a slouched position you are actually making your stomach muscles lazier and thus promoting that shape of abdominal muscles? Not a good habit to have. By walking straight you are actually working your abs.

Posture is a matter of habit

You must concentrate on maintaining a straight posture all the time. Focus on keeping a good posture when you walk, when you sit and when you stand. Posture is also very important when you eat because it helps food pass through your digestive system easier than if you were slouched. Chewing your food better can contribute to the reduction or better yet, prevention, of digestion or acid reflux related issues.

Also, *consider that no matter how hard you work and how good a body you may have, if you slouch, you just ruined the picture (the image of yourself and what you project to others) and made all that effort become almost unnoticed.* For this specific reason, I want to remind you how vital it is to concentrate, work on and make a habit of standing, sitting and walking with a straight posture.

Key points to having a better posture are:

1. Your Shoulders should be relaxed and below your neck height.
2. Your Chest should be out and shoulders back.
3. Your Head needs to be perpendicular to the ground. (Imagine drawing a straight line from your chin to the ground.)
4. Your Eyes should be focused on the horizon NOT on the ground.

Below are examples of different postures that will help making our point.

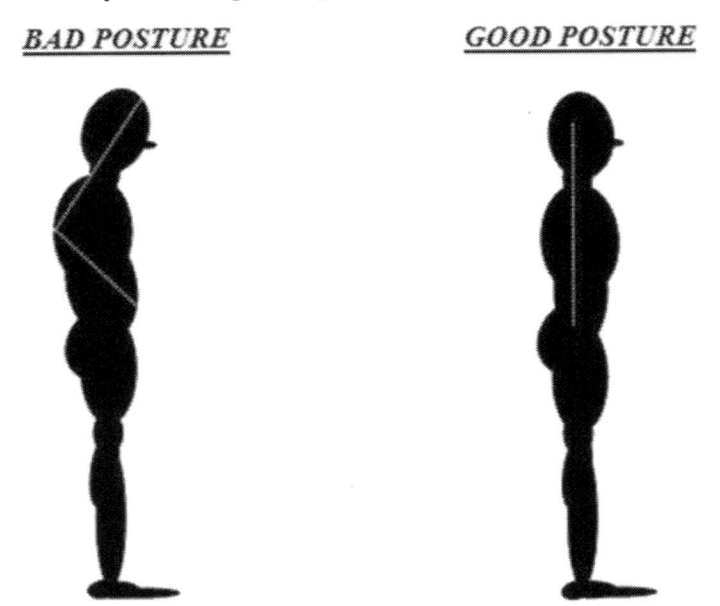

BAD POSTURE   GOOD POSTURE

The first drawing shows how keeping your head facing down actually promotes a bent over posture. The second drawing shows a perfectly straight standing posture and should be what you look like when you are standing straight.

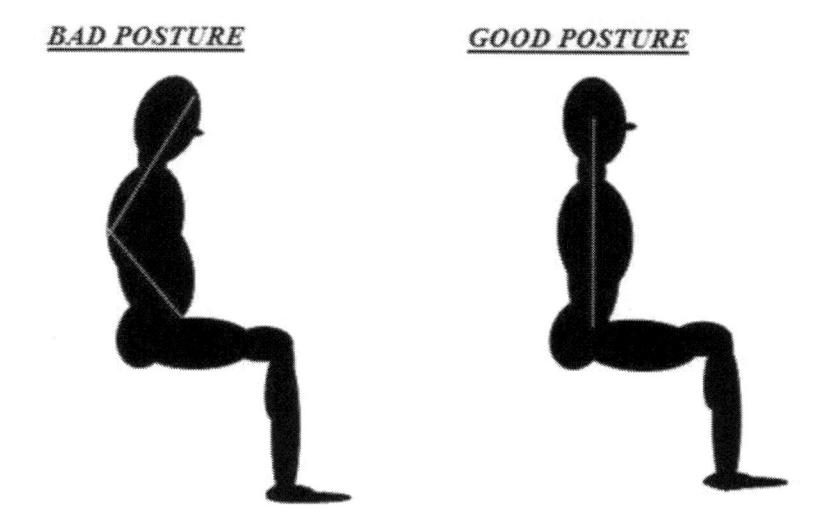

BAD POSTURE   **GOOD POSTURE**

The first drawing shows an example of how not to sit down as you can see from the inclined posture and the abdominal area bent forward. The second drawing shows a perfectly straight posture while facing forward and with the abdominal area tucked in.

BAD POSTURE   **GOOD POSTURE**

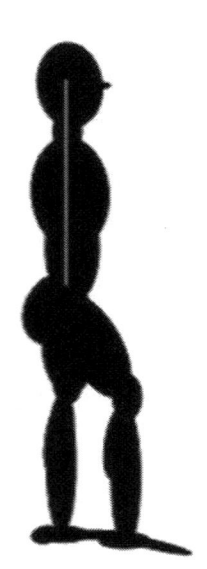

The first drawing shows an improper walking posture with a bent over back while facing downward. The second drawing shows the proper walking position you should be in, with a straight back and facing forward. Notice that the abdominal area is not bending outwards as it is in the first drawing.

CHAPTER 5

YOU ARE WHAT YOU EAT

Commit to improving your mind and body

Does that sound strange to you? "You are what you eat". It's a simple statement with a lot of meaning. What you do during the day or for a living determines what types of activities you physically and mentally do. You become a more active or sedentary person depending on how you spend your time and what you eat. This determines who you are at the end.

Changing your habits

Change your habits by changing your dietary, mental, and physical lifestyle. <u>This means being able to do the same things you already do but now replacing some foods with healthier and</u>

more organic ones. As time goes by you'll feel stronger, more flexible and full of energy because the nutrients you feed your body. *How do you go from eating junk food to healthy food?* This is basically obtained, through discipline and consistency. Use daily food schedule included in the first chapters of this book as guideline to get you there.. With time you will turn eating right into an every day habit and that should be one of your primary goals.

Making the best of your particular situation

Never feel bad about yourself. There's always some else in a worse situation. If you have a bad back and its hurts when you walk, then there's probably someone who can't walk at all so be thankful. If you have knee problems, instead of complaining be happy you have legs. These examples are a little drastic but to the point. If want to get started, you have to make sure you have no excuses so that you don't stop with any excuse. If your back hurts, swim. If your knees hurt, strengthen them or work on your upper body. If your shoulder hurts, work on your abdominals or legs. Learn to improvise.

Different climate

If you live in a place where the weather is terrible you don't really have to worry too much because most of these exercises can be done indoors as well. If it's hot outside then take advantage of the pool exercises. If it's cold outside do the indoor exercises. Just don't stay still

If you feel that having a better nutritional plan or diet is expensive

If this is your case try to find alternatives to the foods described in this book. Instead of going to a major supermarket, try going to a discount food store or food store that sells in bulk. If you plan on sticking to the diet you should have what you need for months to come so you might as well buy in bulk if it works to your advantage cost wise. Another way to economize is to find a training partner to work with you and who can share the costs of food, if that becomes the case. Never let money become the reason for not being in better shape or being healthy!

Remind yourself to train and stick with this nutritional plan

An easy way to remind yourself that you have to train and stick with the nutritional plan is to carry this book around. That way you have the exercises on hand at any time. Another great way to remind yourself that you need to train eat at the right times is to wear a watch with an alarm on it to remind you every hour or every three hours that you need to be taking care of yourself. If you get tired of your watch, I have another great way to remind yourself. Try placing your training shoes or clothes on the floor next to your bed or at the door. Every time you wake up or are simply walking to the door, you will see your shoes and will remember what you need to be doing. If you left your shoes and clothes at the door, you would know you should not be leaving the room until you are done with your training. You have to prepare to succeed and this is how you do it. Help yourself by doing these little things that make a big difference every day.

Remind yourself to resist distractions

Go to the refrigerator and take out all of the food that you should not be eating. Clean the entire refrigerator if need be. Organize the shelves so that you know what you are supposed to eat for breakfast, lunch, and dinner. Make it easy for yourself to eat what you know you should be eating. Keep only fresh food as you don't want to get sick. A lot of people have refrigerators full of food they stocked up months ago and haven't taken the time to throw out expired food. In the refrigerator, keep fruits and vegetables in Ziploc® bags and in lower compartments to make sure they last fresh for as long as possible. <u>Place your dietary plan on the outside of the refrigerator, in your room and in your office to keep you focused.</u>

Don't let others bring you down

You should become your best fan, cheering and pushing hard every day to stick to the diet and exercise plan. If you have others telling you that you won't last on the diet or that you won't continue doing the training routine, stay away from these people. If you can't stay away from these people, learn to separate the noise in what they say from what is actually valuable to you. You have radio and TV commercials as well as shows and some static. Do you focus on the static, the music or the commercials? The same thing will happen in life. You will always have someone who makes a comment just to impose their ideas or their negativity. Don't argue; instead find people who want to accomplish the same things you are trying to accomplish. Search for people who can help you stay focused and truly want you to be successful. Surround yourself with positive, uplifting, and motivated people. Even if others bring you down, show them you can and will make it through this diet. Prove to your kids that you can do anything you set your mind on no matter how difficult it may seem.

When you feel that you lack motivation, I want you to read this to yourself:

- ✓ I will complete my workout today.
- ✓ I will stick to my diet and will not deviate from it.
- ✓ I am the only one who can decide if I am successful or not.
- ✓ It is my responsibility to follow through on my training and diet.
- ✓ I can do it, therefore I will do it.
- ✓ I am the result of my actions.
- ✓ I believe in myself and in my potential.

By reading this to yourself you'll feel a lot better and it will show in your actions!

Write down 10 reasons why you believe you will be successful in completing this diet and exercise routine:

1.

2.

3.

4.

5.

6.

7.

8.

9.

10.

When you're having a bad day read what you just wrote above. Think about what was going through your mind when you wrote these 10 reasons and what you should be thinking right now. Everyone has good and bad days. The key is to get past the bad days in the best possible way so that the good days are that much better. Remember, the results you have today will be the product of efforts made in days before.

Write down 5 physical changes you want to see in your body once completing this diet and exercise routine:

1.

2.

3.

4.

5.

Write down 5 mental or emotional changes your want to reach upon completing this diet and exercise routine:

(ex. I want to be more positive, I want to feel happier about myself and my appearance, I want to have less stress in my life, I want to feel I have more energy every day, etc.)

1.

2.

3.

4.

5.

Write down 10 goals you have for yourself regarding exercise, nutrition, and your life in general. Completing this diet and exercise plan should be a part of your general goals:

1.

2.

3.

4.

5.

6.

7.

8.

9.

10.

CHAPTER 6

THE SECRET TO HAVING THE BEST ABS EVER

Get the Look You Want

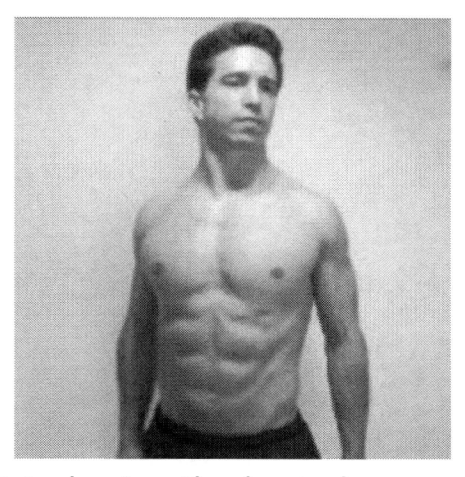

The secret to having the best abs ever is variety. You have to understand that your abdominal muscles are organized in different quadrants that require different types of exercises to get the maximum results out of them. Your core is vital no matter what your sport so you should take the time to work on it often.

Your _Upper abdominal area_ is the easier to define at the beginning because it shapes into form by doing most abdominal exercises.

Lateral area abs (Oblique), are basically the sides around your waist area and these help you to pronounce all the other abdominal areas when you work them hard.

The _mid section_ is an area between your upper abdominal area and your lower abdominal area which look great once they are defined and tight. They are the center piece of your abdominal area.

The hardest section to form is your _lower abdominal area_. These require more leg intensive exercises such as: walking, running, swimming, roller skating, skiing, jumping, etc. Aerobic type workouts make a difference on your lower abs and your overall body. Your lower back muscles are an important component of all core workouts.

Why is that? Basically, when you only work on your abdominal section, your muscles tend to pull you forward and incline you towards hunching your back. By working on your _lower back_ you balance the muscle pull created by your abdominals when you've worked them out and this help your body get in the right posture (which should be straight!). This in turn helps your abs because now they will be nice and straight and not lagging down.

Breathing as you do your abdominal exercises is an important factor in getting fast results. Working on your breathing helps you work most of your abdominal muscles. This can help you get tighter and more toned abs with time. Try to breathe out as you tighten your abs on every abdominal repetition you do.

Every abdominal repetition you do while breathing out will count for three or four abs done without breathing out which equates to having doing less abs and still getting the same results.

Your body will definitely thank you for being more efficient.

I am a firm believer in cross-training which is doing other sports or activities to help you main sport improve. That's why I would suggest cross-training with other sports that you enjoy but that won't get you injured. Swimming is vital because of the amount of abdominal muscles that are stretched and pulled when swim. People that have had knee injuries or leg pain or other related problems can spend more time in the swimming pool and get the same or even better results than without.

Combining upper abdominal workouts with lower abdominal workouts will help you get well defined abdominal muscles but you still have to make sure you take care of your lateral abs and lower back. Working too much on your abs and not enough on your back will cause an imbalance in the amount of pull they create and this can tend to make you slouch when you sit or stand so make sure you train enough back exercises as well. By combining exercises that use all of your abdominal muscles, you will create a strong core section but remember that good cardio exercises will help you lose body fat the fastest. Doing intense cardio exercise and combining abdominal exercises will bring about faster results.

Stretching is an excellent way to prevent injuries and help you shape your body. Shaping your body the way you want it to look requires doing some form of stretching, plus you won't look and feel stiff. I have found that stretching before and after workouts help to prevent soreness, specially the day after a workout so take the time to stretch as well. The stretching exercises I described in the last chapter are very good for your body. You should try them out at your own pace and move up gradually to increased flexibility levels.

Remember to take one day a week off to let your muscles recover. If you feel you need to take a day off every other day, which is fine as well because this is a gradual improvement, then do so. Taking a step forward every day is the key to getting results. One step forward is better than three forward and then getting injured and having to take four steps back with nothing to show.

This is not a race so make sure to complete the workout at your own pace not at someone else's pace!

The best way to train abdominal muscles is to do circuits. Abdominal circuit training means doing different abdominal exercises and then repeating these in subsequent sets. A visual representation will be provided in the following pages. By constantly changing each abdominal exercise you are allowing different abdominal muscles to rest while you work on another group of muscles.

My Favorite Abdominal Workout

1. Scissor abs
2. Heels up and hands behind your head and then go up.
3. Up, up, up and then hips up and back down again.
4. Side, side and center all the way up.
5. Side laterals with knee and elbow up.
6. Back rows facing down.
7. Arms and legs stretched out and then come together facing up.

Do 15 repetitions of each and repeat the entire routine 3 times. As you feel more comfortable with the routine try increasing the repetitions to 20 or more and increase the number of times you complete the routine to 5.

Make sure to stretch your abdominal muscles and back with these three stretches at the end of the entire routine:

1. Abdominal stretch
2. Back stretch
3. Side stretch

Once you are done stretching keep a straight posture during the day as to accustom your core muscles to maintain proper form. A lot of people work their core muscles and then walk away slouching which becomes counter-productive. Do not make this mistake. Maintain a good posture and you will see faster results!

1. Scissor kick abs

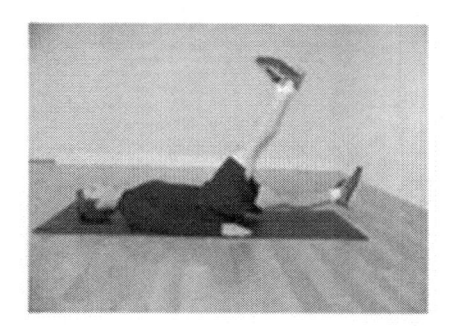

2. Heels up and hands behind head and then go up

3. Up, up, and then hips up and then back down

4. Side, side and center all the way up

5. Side laterals with knee and elbow up

6. Back rows facing down

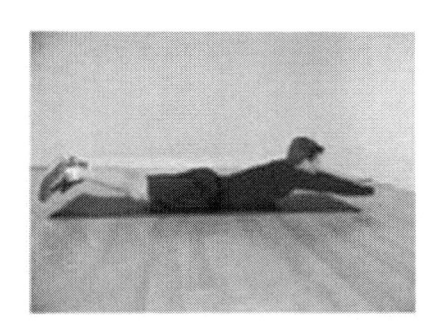

7. Arms and legs stretched out and then come together facing up

Stretches to end the routine:

1. Abdominal stretch

2. Back stretch

3. Side stretch